A Day in the Life of A Crayon

Crayon
Crayon
Crayon
Crayon
Crayon
Crayon

Meg Greve

EZ READERS
AN IMPRINT OF
MITCHELL LANE PUBLISHERS

CREATING YOUNG NONFICTION READERS

EZ Readers offer nonfiction for beginning readers in PreK through first grade, using simple language, clear illustrations, and engaging facts to build vocabulary and confidence.

TIPS FOR READING NONFICTION WITH BEGINNING READERS

Talk about Nonfiction

Begin by explaining that nonfiction books give us information that is true. The book will be organized around a specific topic or idea, and we may learn new facts through reading.

Look at the Parts

Most nonfiction books have helpful features. Our *EZ Readers* include color photographs and graphic aids, a table of contents, a glossary, and an index. Share the purpose of these features with your reader.

Color Photos and Graphic Aids

A lot of information can be found by "reading" photos, charts, maps, and other graphic aids found within nonfiction texts. Help your reader learn more about the different ways information can be displayed.

Table of Contents

Located at the front of the book, this list shows the big ideas within the text and the page numbers where they can be found.

Glossary

Located at the back of the book, the glossary defines key words and phrases that are related to the topic. These words and phrases can be found in the text in colored type.

Index

Located at the back of the book, an index is an alphabetical list of topics and the page numbers where they can be found.

With a little help and guidance about reading nonfiction, you can feel good about introducing a young reader to the world of *EZ Readers* nonfiction books.

EZ Readers is an imprint of:

Mitchell Lane
PUBLISHERS
2001 SW 31st Avenue
Hallandale, FL 33009
mitchelllanepub.com

First Edition, 2027.

Author: Meg Greve
Designer: Rhea Magaro
Editor: Kim Thompson

Library of Congress Cataloging-in-Publication Data
Title: A Day in the Life of a Crayon / by Meg Greve

Description: Hallandale, FL :
Mitchell Lane Publishers, [2027]

Identifiers:
ISBN 979-8-89260-843-5 (library bound)
ISBN 979-8-89260-933-3 (eBook)

Library of Congress Control Number: 2025950824

PHOTO CREDITS
Alamy: Jerry Editor, 13, 22; Shutterstock: Mega Pixel, 5; Yellow Cat, 5; tomeqs, 7; InveStock, 8; New Africa, 10; PeopleImages, 14; angelbandala, 17, 22; Satakorn, 18; Jammy Photography, 21, 22; Ljupco Smokovski, 22; MargJohnsonVA, 22.

Table of Contents

I Am a Crayon

I am made of **wax**.

I wear a paper **jacket**.

BY THE WAY...
I live in a box with
my friends. We are
many colors.

Good morning!

The school bell rings.

Yay! It is time to color!

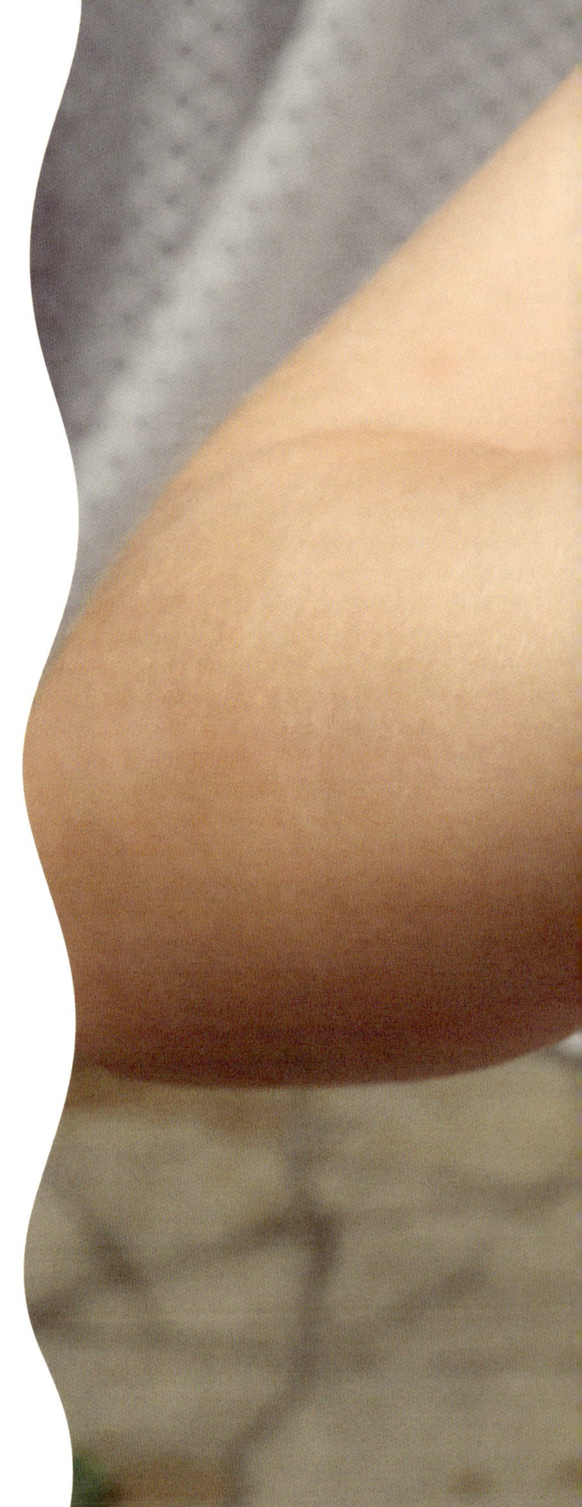

BY THE WAY...
Please pick me out of the box!

PULAU PANDAN
Oil Pastel

A hand reaches for me.

I color animals. I color the sky.

I glide across the page.

BY THE WAY...
Please keep me on your paper.

Once, I colored a desk.

I colored a wall.

I did not like it.
(Not one bit!)

My **point** wears down.

Peel back my paper.

You can keep using me.

BY THE WAY...

Please throw the paper in the trash, not on the floor.

More hands want me.

If you need *blue*, do not feel *blue*. Your turn will come.

(See? I made a joke!)

The table gets
bumped.

I **roll** and roll.

Oh, no, I am falling!

peach
durazno
Crayola.com
Crayola
Crayola.com
gray
gris
Crayola
Crayola.com

BY THE WAY...
Be careful! Do not trip on me.

On the floor, I see some friends.

We wait.

Please, please pick us up!

The school bell rings again.

We snuggle into our box.

It is time to close the **lid**.

(What a day! I need to rest.)

BY THE WAY...

See you tomorrow!

Glossary

colors (KUH-lurz) red, blue, green, yellow, and other hues that people can see

jacket (JAK-it) an outer covering

lid (lid) a top or cover for a container

peel (peel) to pull off a strip of something

point (point) the sharp end of something

roll (rohl) to move by turning over and over

trip (trip) to fall or almost fall because you hit your foot on something

wax (waks) a hard substance made of oils and fats and used in candles and crayons

Quiz Me

1. When I peel paper from a crayon, I throw it away.

   A. Yes B. No

2. I only color on paper, not on desks or walls.

   A. Yes B. No

3. I share crayons with others.

   A. Yes B. No

4. I pick up crayons and put them away.

   A. Yes B. No

ANSWER KEY:

How many times did you answer yes?

4: Awesome! You take great care of your crayons.
3: Great! You are ready to make colorful pictures.
2: That's okay! Keep learning and practicing.
1: You're starting to learn. Keep trying!

Further Reading

Jones, Jennifer. *Crayons on Strike.* Random Source, 2022.

Koch, Alli. *How to Draw All the Things for Kids.* Paige Tate and Company, 2020.

On the Internet

Mental Floss: 10 Colorful Facts about Coloring Books
mentalfloss.com/fun/10-colorful-facts-about-coloring-books
Learn more about coloring books and how they came to be.

PBS: Mr. Rogers' Neighborhood: How People Make Crayons
pbs.org/video/mister-rogers-neighborhood-competition-how-people-make-crayons
Watch crayons being made in a factory.

Index

About the Author

Meg Greve has been in education for more than 30 years. She still loves to color with crayons. When she was little, her favorite color was sky blue. It came out of a box with 64 colors. The box even had a sharpener. Her favorite picture to draw was the ocean and all the animals that live in it!